Anne Frank
Voice of Hope

Cath Senker

H O D D E R
Wayland

an imprint of Hodder Children's Books

© 2000 White-Thomson Publishing Ltd

Produced for Hodder Wayland by
White-Thomson Publishing Ltd
2/3 St Andrew's Place, Lewes, BN7 1UP

Editor: Liz Gogerly
Cover Design: Jan Sterling
Inside Design: Joyce Chester
Picture Research: Shelley Noronha – Glass Onion Pictures
Proofreader: Alison Cooper

Cover: Anne Frank in 1942
Title page: Anne at school aged about 11

Published in Great Britain in 2000 by Hodder Wayland,
a division of Hodder Children's Books

Titles in this series:
Fidel Castro: Leader of Cuba's Revolution
Diana: The People's Princess
Anne Frank: Voice of Hope
Nelson Mandela: Father of Freedom
Mother Teresa: Saint of the Slums
Muhammad Ali: The Greatest
Pope John Paul II: Pope for the People
The Queen Mother: Grandmother of a Nation

A Catalogue record for this book is available from the
British Library

ISBN 0 7502 3047 9

Printed and bound in Italy by G. Canale & C.S.p.A.

Hodder Children's Books
A division of Hodder Headline Limited
338 Euston Road, London, NW1 3BH

Picture Acknowledgements
The publisher would like to thank the following for their
kind permission to use these pictures:
AKG, London 4, 10, 16, 18, 19, 21 (left and right), 23, 26,
27, 28, 30, 31, 34, 35, 36, 38, 40, 41, 45; Anne Frank
House Museum (AFF/AFS) 19, 20, 22, 24, 29, 43, 44
(bottom); Archive Photos Anne Frank Fonds, Basel/Anne
Frank House 13; Associated Press 7, 9; Hodder Wayland
Picture Library 5/ ©Keystone 14/ © National Film Archive
32/ 39; Popperfoto 10, 15, 33, 37, 44 (top); Topham
Picturepoint (*cover*), (*title page*), 6, 12, 17, 23 (top and
bottom), 25 (top and bottom), 42

Leisure & Community Services

Please return this item by the last date stamped below, to the library from which it was borrowed.

Renewals
You may renew any item twice (for 3 weeks) by telephone or post, providing it is not required by another reader. *Please quote the number stated below.*

Overdue charges
Please see library notices for the current rate of charges for overdue items. Overdue charges are not made on junior books unless borrowed on adult tickets.

Postage
Both adult and junior borrowers must pay any postage on overdue notices.

26 OCT 2002	1 1 OCT 2008		
16.11.02 FMB			
27 SEP 2003	2 7 AUG 2015		
01 NOV 2003			
0 4 NOV 2006	– 8 APR 2023		
– 8 MAR 2007			
2 2 SEP 2007			
2 2 MAR 2008			

739.96

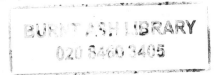
Bromley
THE LONDON BOROUGH

BROMLEY LIBRARIES

3 0128 02344 6779

Contents

Disappearing at Dawn 4

Anne is Born 6

Jewish People under Attack 8

'Jews Out!' 10

'Ordinary Life' in Amsterdam 12

Jews not Welcome 14

The Secret Plan 16

Last Months of Freedom 18

The Secret Annexe 20

Life behind the Secret Bookcase 22

Problems, Arguments and Boredom 24

When Will it all End? 26

Anne Falls in Love 28

'I Want to be a Writer' 30

'The Gestapo is Here' 32

Kamp Westerbork 34

The Horror of Auschwitz 36

Rescue Comes too Late 38

Otto's Story 40

Anne Frank's Diary 42

The Anne Frank House 44

Glossary 46

Date Chart 47

Further Information 47

Index 48

Disappearing at Dawn

It was 5.30 in the morning on 6 July 1942. Otto and Edith Frank, and their daughters Margot and Anne, awoke and hurriedly put on several layers of clothes. 'No Jew in our situation would dare leave the house with a suitcase full of clothes,' wrote Anne later. The girls grabbed their satchels. Margot left on her bicycle with Miep, a trusted friend who worked for Otto. The rest of the family followed at 7.30. The only living creature Anne said goodbye to was her cat, Moortje. As they walked in the rain, Otto and Edith explained the hiding plan to Anne.

'I stuck the craziest things in the satchel, but I'm not sorry. Memories mean more to me than dresses.'
Anne Frank's Diary.

Pictures from Anne Frank's photo album show the happy times the Franks left behind.

The day before, Margot had received a call-up saying she was to be sent to a concentration camp. Fearing Margot would be killed if she went, the Franks were going to the hiding place they had been secretly preparing, to escape from the Nazis.

Hidden away in the Secret Annexe for the next two years, Anne wrote the diary that was to make her world famous.

Jewish people in Amsterdam, summer 1943. The Nazis forced Jews to wear a yellow star to mark them out from other people.

Anne is Born

Otto with Margot and Anne in 1930. Otto spent lots of time with his girls and loved making up bedtime stories for them.

When baby Anne was born on 12 June 1929, her parents, Otto and Edith Frank, were proud and delighted. They hoped their new daughter would have a happy and comfortable future. No one could imagine the terror that was to strike them just a few years later.

This photo from 1957 shows the house where the Franks lived in Frankfurt.

'I cannot claim that I did not feel Jewish at the time. But somehow I was quite consciously German. Otherwise, I would never have become an officer during World War I.' Otto Frank.

Otto and Edith's families were Jewish, and had lived in Germany for many generations. Otto's mother could trace her family back to the sixteenth century. The Franks felt German as well as Jewish. Otto fought for Germany in the First World War, as did 100,000 other German Jews, and he became an officer in the army.

The Franks lived in a friendly neighbourhood of Frankfurt where there were plenty of children for Anne and her older sister Margot to play with. There were Catholics and Protestants as well as Jews. Sometimes the Franks invited their non-Jewish neighbours to celebrate the Jewish holiday of Hanukkah with them. They all got on well together, whatever their religion.

Jewish People under Attack

In 1929, the German economy collapsed, and millions of people lost their jobs. Many people looked to the Socialist party or the Communist party to sort out these problems, but the two parties would not work together. The Nazi party, led by Adolf Hitler, took the opportunity to gain support. Hitler promised he would create jobs for everyone, and told the better-off people he would stop the communists.

A synagogue being burnt down in Germany, in November 1938, as part of the campaign against the Jews.

'I don't like it. I don't know what's going to happen. I'm scared of the Right.' Otto Frank talking about politics, remembered by his English cousin, Milly Stanfield.

Anne Frank out shopping with her mother and sister, 1933. The photo was taken by Otto in the Hauptwache, a famous square in Frankfurt.

The Nazis hated the communists, but they also blamed Germany's problems on people they said weren't German – black people, homosexuals, Romanies (Gypsies) and, especially, Jews. The Nazis said that the Jews were sucking all the wealth out of Germany. Yet Jews only formed one per cent of the population, and few of them were rich.

In the early 1930s, there were more and more attacks on Jews by Nazis. Frankfurt, where Anne's family lived, was home to 30,000 Jews. Otto and Edith became worried, although they tried to carry on life as normal.

'Jews Out!'

In January 1933, the Nazis were elected as the main party in government, and, in March, Hitler seized total power. In Frankfurt, the Nazis won control of the town council. They celebrated on the steps of the town hall, waving flags with swastikas and yelling, 'Jews out!'

In the following months, laws were passed against Jews and other groups, such as black people, homosexuals and Romanies. Many Jews were forced out of their jobs, all trade unions were closed down, and books by Jews, communists and gay people were ripped up and burnt. Jewish children were thrown out of non-Jewish schools.

Below **Nazis loading books on to a truck to be taken to a book burning, Berlin, 1933.**

Above **Adolf Hitler addressing his followers. The Nazis held huge meetings to show their strength.**

A picture from an anti-Semitic children's book, showing Jewish children being forced to leave school. All the Jewish people are shown to be ugly.

Margot had to leave her school, and Anne would not be able to start nursery in September 1933 as planned. The Nazis brought in new schoolbooks showing Jews as monsters. At break time, children played the latest board game – 'Jews Out!'

The Frank family thought it was time to leave Germany.

'I lived in Frankfurt until I was four. Because we're Jewish, my father emigrated to Holland [the Netherlands] in 1933.'
Anne Frank's Diary.

'Ordinary Life' in Amsterdam

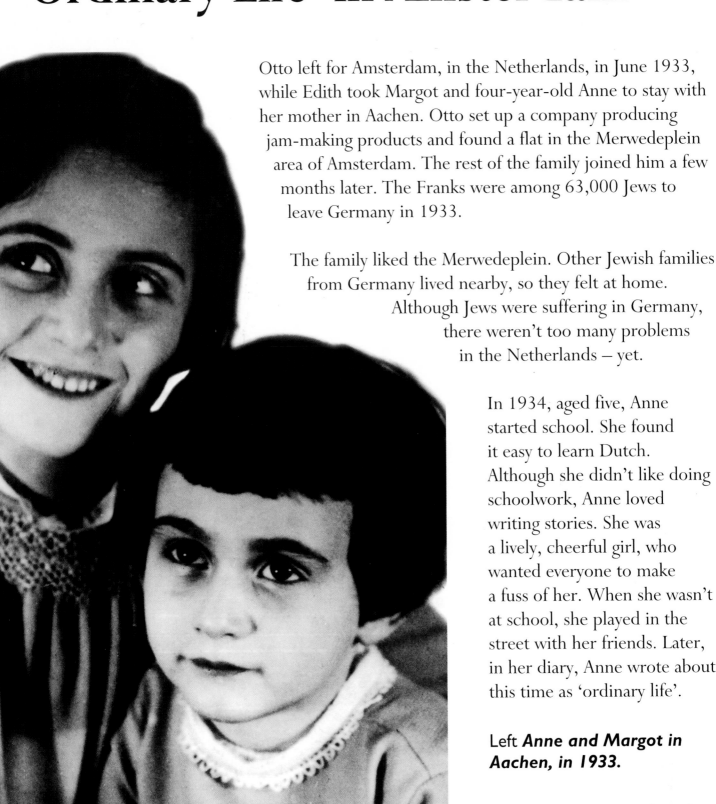

Otto left for Amsterdam, in the Netherlands, in June 1933, while Edith took Margot and four-year-old Anne to stay with her mother in Aachen. Otto set up a company producing jam-making products and found a flat in the Merwedeplein area of Amsterdam. The rest of the family joined him a few months later. The Franks were among 63,000 Jews to leave Germany in 1933.

The family liked the Merwedeplein. Other Jewish families from Germany lived nearby, so they felt at home. Although Jews were suffering in Germany, there weren't too many problems in the Netherlands – yet.

In 1934, aged five, Anne started school. She found it easy to learn Dutch. Although she didn't like doing schoolwork, Anne loved writing stories. She was a lively, cheerful girl, who wanted everyone to make a fuss of her. When she wasn't at school, she played in the street with her friends. Later, in her diary, Anne wrote about this time as 'ordinary life'.

Left **Anne and Margot in Aachen, in 1933.**

Right **Anne and her friend Sanne in Amsterdam, 1935.**

'Margot went on to Holland [the Netherlands] in December, and I followed in February, and was put on Margot's table as a birthday present.'
Anne Frank's Diary.

Jews not Welcome

Anne on the flat roof at the back of the Franks' home in the Merwedeplein, summer 1940.

In September 1939, the Second World War broke out. In the countries ruled by Germany, life for Jews was terrible. They lost all their freedoms, and the Nazi government started to send them away to workcamps.

In May 1940, the Nazis took over the Netherlands. For a few weeks at first, people didn't notice much difference. Anne's life carried on as normal. Now twelve, she loved to wear stylish clothes and was always careful to look her best. Her first boyfriend was Peter Schiff, described by Anne as 'very good-looking... when he laughed a naughty glint came into his eyes.'

But, from June 1940, new laws came in to separate Jews from non-Jews. Soon, Jews were not allowed to work or study with non-Jews. Jewish children found they could not visit cafés, cinemas or swimming pools. In the summer of 1941, Anne and Margot had to leave the school they loved to go to a Jewish school. The Netherlands was becoming just like Germany.

> '*After May 1940 the good times were few and far between: first there was the war, then the capitulation [surrender] and then the arrival of the Germans, which is when the trouble started for the Jews.*' Anne Frank's Diary.

Germans who mixed with Jews were insulted in public.

The Secret Plan

In the summer of 1941, the Nazis were plotting to kill all the Jews in Europe. Some Jews had managed to escape to Britain or the United States but, by 1941, many families were trapped in Nazi-occupied Europe.

Otto Frank started to prepare a hiding place above his offices. The staff helped him, even though they risked prison or death for aiding Jews. Otto did not tell the children about the plan; he wanted them to enjoy their last few months of freedom.

Jewish people working in a clothing factory in Warsaw, Poland, in about 1941. Some three million Polish Jews were killed by the Nazis during the course of the war.

*Anne at school, aged
about eleven.*

But life was getting difficult for Jewish children too. All
bicycles had to be handed in and, because Jews were not
allowed to use the buses and trams, children now had to walk
everywhere. More frighteningly, friends and family were
being taken away to concentration camps. Jacque, one of
Anne's friends, remembered her cousin being sent away.
He was never seen again.

Last Months of Freedom

By May 1942, the underground newspapers reported horrifying stories of Jews being gassed to death in Auschwitz concentration camp in Poland. The following month, even more severe laws were passed against Jews in the Netherlands. Then the Nazi Government made the chilling announcement that, starting from July, all of them would be sent to concentration camps.

The Jews of the Warsaw Ghetto (Jewish area) rose up against their Nazi rulers in 1943. They fought bravely but could not beat the Nazis. Here they are shown after they have surrendered.

'I hope I will be able to confide everything to you, as I have never been able to confide in anyone.'
Anne Frank's Diary.

A prisoner in Auschwitz concentration camp. The camp was built for killing people. As many as 12,000 people a day were killed there.

The diary Anne received on her birthday. She had chosen it herself.

On 12 June, it was Anne's thirteenth birthday. Among her presents was a diary, which she named Kitty. Anne felt that she didn't have anyone she could really talk to, and she wanted her diary to be a real friend. She poured out all her thoughts and feelings to Kitty – about schoolfriends, exam results, and her new boyfriend, Hello Silberberg.

A few weeks later, on 5 July, Margot received a notice saying she was to be sent to a German workcamp. The Frank family went into hiding immediately. One of the few things Anne crammed into her satchel was her diary.

The Secret Annexe

The main photograph shows Auguste and Hermann van Pels. In the background is a picture of their son, Peter. The Franks and the van Pelses did not know each other very well until they went into hiding together.

The hiding place was above Otto's office at 263 Prinsengracht. Office workers Victor Kugler, Johannes Kleiman, Miep Gies and Bep Voskuijl were part of the secret plan. They had agreed to help the Franks despite the terrible danger of discovery.

On 13 July, the van Pels family arrived – Hermann, Auguste and their 15-year-old son Peter. Fritz Pfeffer joined them in November. The eight people in the Secret Annexe lived together as one big family.

The outside of 263 Prinsengracht in 1950, when the building was in need of repair.

The bookcase that hid the entrance to the Secret Annexe. Visitors to the offices below knew nothing of the rooms above them.

Keeping 'as quiet as baby mice' was the key to survival. During the day, the families had to walk quietly and talk softly so that no one in the office below could hear them. Anne and Otto made curtains so that neighbours could not see in. Bep's father cleverly made a bookcase to cover up the entrance to the Annexe.

When the office was closed, the Annexe dwellers could creep downstairs to bathe in private and peer out of the window. But they could never go out.

Life behind the Secret Bookcase

'Bep gives Margot and me a lot of office work; it makes us both feel important and is a great help to her.'
Anne Frank's Diary.

The families in hiding studied to pass the time. The young people kept up their schoolwork, learnt new languages, and even took a course in shorthand. Anne read widely and took comfort in writing her diary.

A visit from one of the helpers brought huge excitement. As well as a fresh face to talk to, they brought news of the outside world, newspapers and library books.

Otto with the people who gave most help to the families in hiding: (left to right) Miep Gies, Johannes Kleiman, Otto Frank, Victor Kugler and Bep Voskuijl.

Bottles of lemonade and foods such as butter and cheese were luxuries to the Annexe dwellers.

The biggest difficulty for the helpers was finding food. They had to buy most of it on the black market. Many of the arguments in the Annexe were about the quality of the meals – or about who was being too greedy.

The Annexe dwellers did all kinds of work to repay their friends' kindness, from doing the office accounts to filling packets of food and stoning cherries.

Problems, Arguments and Boredom

A lively, fun-loving girl of thirteen, Anne found it incredibly hard to live cooped up indoors with no friends of her own age. She felt she was unfairly picked on by everyone else because she was the youngest. Sometimes, Anne didn't get on with her mother at all and often said she hated her – 'she doesn't even know what I think about the most ordinary things'. Margot was the golden girl, receiving nothing but praise. Anne loved her father the most, but thought that he didn't support her enough when the others shouted at her.

Anne's room. The pictures on the walls have remained there since the families lived in the Annexe.

In her diary, Anne describes Peter as rather dull, but she saves her rudest remarks for Mrs van Pels, who appears vain and stupid. Mrs van Pels was constantly complaining to Anne's parents about her cheekiness.

Everyone was living under terrible stress. It was so boring in hiding, and yet there was the constant fear of being discovered and sent to the death camps.

The Annexe toilet. No one was allowed to flush it during the day in case visitors heard the noise.

The wall of Anne's room, with her favourite film stars, and English princesses Elizabeth and Margaret Rose (one above the other).

'If I just think of how we live here, I usually come to the conclusion that it is a paradise compared with how other Jews who are not in hiding must be living.'
Anne Frank's Diary.

When Will it all End?

In September 1943, the families in hiding heard the best news from the war so far. Italy had surrendered and the British had landed in Naples. They all hoped this would bring the end of the war closer. But daily life became no easier.

By the autumn of 1943, Anne was desperately depressed. She found herself in the middle of arguments the whole time – the families argued over everything, especially food. Of course, all the Annexe dwellers were feeling the strain of over a year in hiding. Even the helpers were suffering from poor health because of the stress of helping their friends.

'Sometimes I'm afraid my face is going to sag with all this sorrow and that my mouth is going to permanently droop at the corners.'
Anne Frank's Diary.

British troops landing in Sicily, 10 July 1943. Italy was an ally of Germany, so its surrender was a blow to Hitler.

Everyone was worried about being discovered. What if, after all their efforts, someone were to betray them? They were particularly concerned about one of the warehouse workers, Mr van Maaren, who was becoming rather suspicious about the strange comings and goings of the office staff.

Many Hungarian Jews thought the Nazis would leave them alone, but, in summer 1944, they were sent away to camps, too.

Anne Falls in Love

A photo of Anne from May 1942. There are no photos of the families while they were in hiding.

'Although I'm only fourteen, I know quite well what I want, I know who is right and who is wrong, I have my own opinions, my own ideas and principles...'
Anne Frank's Diary.

By the spring of 1944, Anne realized she was growing up and becoming a young woman. She enjoyed watching her body develop, although she could only share the excitement with her diary because she had no friends of her own age. It was too embarrassing to talk about body changes and sex with her family. Anne was so keen to share the changes in her life with someone that she started to become friendly with Peter van Pels.

Anne had always thought that she and Peter had little in common. But now she got to know him, and they fell in love for a while. They spent time in the attic becoming close to each other; Anne wrote excitedly about her first 'proper' kiss. She told her father about the relationship, but he just told her to be careful. In other ways, Anne felt more grown up too. She was no longer so angry about the difficulties of her life and had come to terms with living in hiding.

Peter van Pels. Anne turned to Peter because she was lonely, but they were only close for a short while.

'I Want to be a Writer'

Some pages from Anne's diaries, written between 1942 and 1944. Anne did not like this photo of herself.

While in the Annexe, Anne realized that she wanted to become a writer. She had started writing short stories as well as her diary. Some were about life in the Annexe, such as 'Villains', which was about the flea problem they suffered. Because the van Pelses didn't use the flea spray, they were the villains of the story – not the fleas.

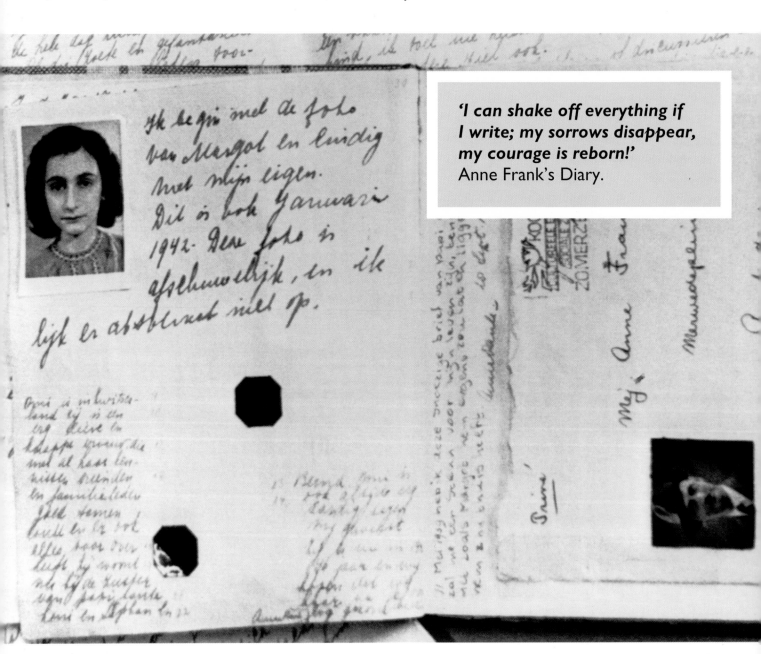

> *'I can shake off everything if I write; my sorrows disappear, my courage is reborn!'*
> Anne Frank's Diary.

Anne knew she wanted to make something of her life. She wrote, 'I must have something besides a husband and children, something that I can devote myself to.' She felt it was unfair that women should just look after their home and family and have no other opportunities.

On 28 March 1944, Gerrit Bolkestein, the Dutch Minister of Education in exile in London, made a speech saying that people's writings about the war would be collected afterwards and shown at a special centre. Anne became sure she wanted to be a journalist. She started to edit her diaries so that they could be published after the war.

The families in hiding were excited by the idea that Anne might publish a book about the Secret Annexe after the war.

'The Gestapo is Here'

Suddenly, the dreaded moment came. On 4 August 1944, a group of Dutch Nazis arrived at the office at 263 Prinsengracht. 'We know everything,' said their leader, Karl Silberbauer. He ordered Kugler to take them to the hidden Jews.

The Nazis pushed their way in through the secret bookcase. Silberbauer was astonished that the group had been in hiding for two years. Otto showed him the pencil marks where they had measured how Anne had grown taller.

A picture from a film made about Anne Frank's diary, showing the arrest of Jewish families.

Dit is een foto, zoals
ik me zou wensen,
altijd zo te zijn.
Dan had ik nog wel
een kans om naar
Holywood te komen.
Anne Frank.
10 Oct. 1942

(translation)
"This is a photo as I would wish
myself to look all the time. Then
I would maybe have a chance to
come to Hollywood."
Anne Frank, 10 Oct. 1942

Shocked and frightened, the eight Annexe dwellers had five minutes to collect a few belongings. The families were bundled into a police van and taken to prison. That evening, Miep and Bep visited the Annexe. There were mounds of books and papers all over the floor. Miep rescued Anne's precious diary papers, a photo album and some books.

On 7 August, Miep went to see Silberbauer to try to bribe him to release the prisoners. He said there was nothing he could do. The following day they were sent to Westerbork transit camp.

A photo of Anne that she stuck in her diary. Miep managed to find Anne's diary but not Margot's.

'I will keep everything... I'll keep everything safely for Anne until she comes back.'
Miep Gies.

Kamp Westerbork

The D-Day landings of June 1944 had given hope to the families in hiding. It seemed that Germany was losing the war. Travelling on the train to Westerbork was almost like an outing after being indoors for two years, although they were locked into the carriages. Perhaps they would just stay at Westerbork until the end of the war.

When they arrived, Anne and the others were sent to the punishment block because they had been in hiding. They could not keep their own clothes, they received less food than the others and they had to work harder.

US troops landing in Normandy, France, on 6 June 1944. The huge Allied invasion force fought to take back France from German control.

> 'Anne was so lovely, so radiant... her movements, her looks, had such a lilt to them... She was happy in Westerbork, though that seems almost incredible.'
> Rosa de Winter, a family friend in Westerbork.

Jewish people in Würzburg, Germany, being sent to the camps in 1942.

Westerbork camp was surrounded by a high, barbed-wire fence. There were wooden barracks, each holding 300 people, where people slept on bunk beds. Men and women were in separate barracks. The camp was a town in itself, with a laundry, school and farm, and all kinds of services such as dental clinics and hairdressers.

Yet, every Tuesday, a group of Jews was selected for transport to the death camps in Poland.

The Horror of Auschwitz

On 3 September, the last train to leave the Netherlands for Auschwitz left Westerbork carrying 1,019 people. The eight from the Annexe were among them.

After three days locked in a cattle truck, they arrived at Auschwitz. The old, sick and very young clambered aboard trucks and were taken straight to the gas chambers. Men and women were separated and forced to march to the camp.

Hungarian Jewish women at Auschwitz, June 1944. Their heads were shaved when they arrived at the camp.

At Auschwitz, Anne rose at 3.30 am, had a slop of brown liquid for breakfast and marched to work. Then, she had to dig an area of grass until 6 pm, with only a half-hour break for lunch. At 6 pm Anne helped to give out the bread in the barracks. Three hours later, she could finally get some sleep.

On 27 October, some women were selected to work in a weapons factory, where there was a better chance of surviving. But Anne had scabies. Margot and Edith would not leave her behind. Margot joined Anne in the scabies block and soon both were seriously ill.

> 'The Frank girls looked terrible. Their hands and bodies were covered with spots and sores from the scabies.'
> Ronnie Goldstein van Cleef, Auschwitz survivor.

Women in Bergen-Belsen concentration camp. It was hard to keep clean in the overcrowded camps and diseases spread quickly.

Rescue Comes too Late

Leaving their mother in Auschwitz, Anne and Margot were moved to Bergen-Belsen concentration camp at the end of October. Edith died on 6 January 1945.

Margot and Anne made friends with Lientje and Janny Brilleslijper. The four girls huddled together to sleep in a huge, filthy tent, lying on straw alongside 200 other women. When the tent blew down in a storm, they were moved to barracks. Conditions there were disgusting; dead bodies were simply left lying on the floor.

People in barracks after they were freed from Bergen-Belsen camp by the British army in April 1945.

In February, Anne met Lies, an old friend from Amsterdam. Anne was cold, hungry and ill, and she believed that both her parents had been killed. Lies managed to give Anne a package of food, but she never saw her again.

In spring 1945, many of the prisoners at Bergen-Belsen caught typhus, Margot and Anne among them. They lay feverish on their bunks, painfully thin and freezing cold. In March, Margot died, followed by Anne a few days later. On 15 April, British troops freed the prisoners of Belsen.

'I always think, if Anne had known that her father was still alive, she might have had more strength to survive.'
Lies Goslar.

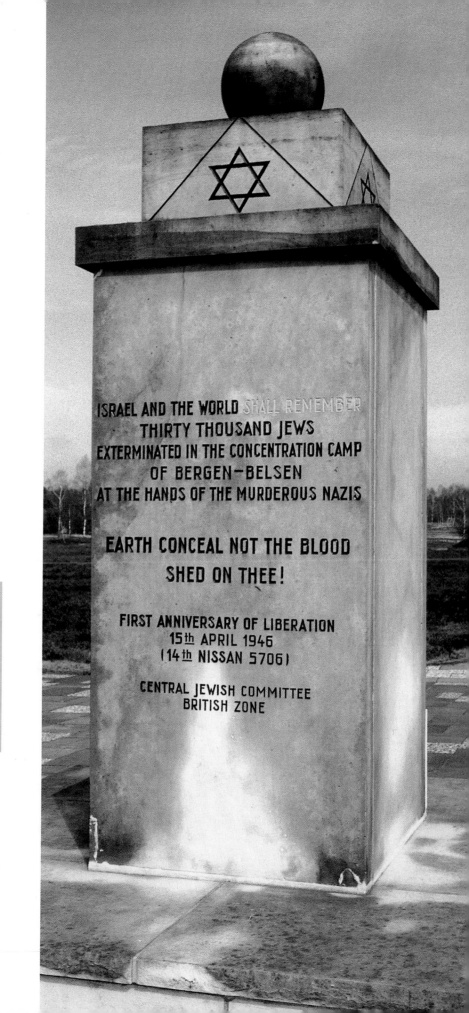

ISRAEL AND THE WORLD SHALL REMEMBER
THIRTY THOUSAND JEWS
EXTERMINATED IN THE CONCENTRATION CAMP
OF BERGEN-BELSEN
AT THE HANDS OF THE MURDEROUS NAZIS

EARTH CONCEAL NOT THE BLOOD
SHED ON THEE!

FIRST ANNIVERSARY OF LIBERATION
15th APRIL 1946
(14th NISSAN 5706)

CENTRAL JEWISH COMMITTEE
BRITISH ZONE

A memorial at Bergen-Belsen, built in memory of those who died there.

Otto's Story

Otto Frank was the only one of the group from the Secret Annexe to survive the war. He was in Auschwitz when the Soviet army freed the prisoners on 27 January 1945.
If Margot and Anne had still been in Auschwitz, perhaps they too would have escaped death.

Now all Otto wanted to do was to return home and find out if any of his family had survived. However, the war had not yet ended in the Netherlands. After travelling to Odessa (on the Black Sea), then by boat to Marseilles, France, and overland to Amsterdam, he arrived back on 3 June.

Survivors of Dachau concentration camp, including children, greet the US troops who have freed them.

Women freed from Bergen-Belsen camp getting new clothes, April 1945.

Otto went straight to see Miep and Jan Gies, who were overjoyed to see him. He knew his wife had died, but now searched daily to find out if his daughters were still alive. Two months later, Otto heard the tragic news that Margot and Anne were dead.

Of about 110,000 Jews who had been sent away from the Netherlands, only 4,700 returned.

'My friends, who had been hopeful with me, now mourned with me.' Otto Frank.

Anne Frank's Diary

Miep had been keeping Anne's diary to give back to her after the war. In sadness, she now gave it to Otto. Otto read the diary and found out for the first time how his daughter was really feeling while they were in hiding.

'I don't want to have lived for nothing like most people... I want to go on living even after my death!'
Anne Frank's diary.

A photo of Otto Frank, taken from Anne's photo album.

Anne Frank's diary has been printed in different languages all over the world.

Otto allowed other people to read parts of Anne's diary, and then tried to find a publisher. No one wanted to publish it so soon after the war, but, in 1947, the diary was finally published in Dutch. Anne's wish to become a writer had come true.

Anne Frank's diary was soon published in French and German. By the 1990s, it had been translated into fifty-five languages. For many people, Anne Frank became a symbol of the six million Jewish people who were murdered by the Nazis. It is hard to understand how such a huge number could be killed, but we can understand one person's story.

The Anne Frank House

After the war, the house where the Franks and the van Pelses had hidden was still used as a business office. Once Anne's diary was published, people used to knock at the door of 263 Prinsengracht to ask if they could look around.

However, by 1957, the building was in such a bad state that there were plans to knock it down. Otto Frank and many others thought that it should be kept open, and a campaign was set up to save the building.

Nelson Mandela speaking at the opening of an Anne Frank exhibition in South Africa in August 1994.

An exhibition, 'Anne Frank: a history for today', held in Amsterdam. Exhibitions such as these can bring history alive for people who did not live through the Second World War themselves.

The Anne Frank House was opened as a museum in 1960. The Annexe was left just how it was after the families were arrested. Each year, about 600,000 people from around the world visit the house. If you go, you'll see exhibitions about the Nazis and about the problems of racism today – as well as the famous diaries.

'On a wall I can still see the lines I drew to show how the children grew. The pictures of film stars that Anne hung up for decoration are still on the wall in her room.'
Otto, visiting the Anne Frank House.

The Anne Frank House in Amsterdam. The front part and the offices where the helpers worked have been returned to the style of the early 1940s. On display are various objects, documents and photos that were rescued after the families were arrested.

Glossary

Annexe A separate or added building, especially to provide extra living space.

Barracks A building used to house large numbers of people, usually soldiers.

Black market The illegal buying and selling of goods that are hard to get hold of in the shops.

Communist party The Communist party in Germany was called the KPD. The communists wanted to make a revolution, like the one that had taken place in Russia.

Concentration camp A huge camp for holding large numbers of prisoners. Millions of people in the Nazi camps were murdered in gas chambers or died from disease and lack of food.

Cooped up To be kept in a small space.

D-Day The day (6 June 1944) when the Allied forces landed on the beaches of northern France to fight the Nazis.

Edit To make corrections to a text.

Gestapo The Nazi secret police.

Hanukkah The Jewish festival of lights which lasts for 8 days in December each year.

Nazis The name for members of the German Nazi Party, the NSDAP. The Nazis believed in a government with total power over the people and wanted to get rid of Jews, homosexuals, black people, Romanies and disabled people.

Published Prepared and printed a book to sell to the public.

Scabies A disease caused by lice burrowing under the skin, forming itchy sores.

Seized Took something from somebody, usually by force.

Shorthand A way of writing quickly using symbols and short forms of words.

Socialist party The Socialist party in Germany, the SPD, believed in making workers' lives better gradually instead of through a violent revolution.

Surrendered Gave up.

Swastika The symbol used by Nazi Germany.

Trade unions Organizations that protect the rights of workers. The Nazis crushed all trade unions because they wanted the government to have all the power.

Transit camp A large camp in which prisoners were kept before transporting them to concentration camps.

Typhus A disease spread by lice and fleas, causing rashes, headaches and fever. It spreads easily where large numbers of people are crowded together and many victims die.

Underground newspapers Newspapers printed and sold secretly because the Nazis allowed no newspapers except their own.

Workcamps The Nazis sent people they wanted to get rid of to camps where they were forced to do hard work for no money.

Date Chart

1929, 12 June Anne Frank is born in Frankfurt, Germany.

1933, June Otto leaves for Amsterdam, the Netherlands; Edith and the children go to Aachen.

1933, December Edith and Margot move to Amsterdam.

1934, February Anne arrives in Amsterdam.

1934 Anne starts school.

1941 Anne and Margot go to the Jewish Lyceum school in Amsterdam.

1942, 12 June Anne receives the diary for her thirteenth birthday.

1942, 6 July The Frank family goes into hiding, followed on the 13th by the van Pels family.

1942, 16 November Fritz Pfeffer joins the families in hiding.

1944, 4 August The families hiding in the Secret Annexe are discovered and, on the 8th, are sent to Westerbork concentration camp.

1944, 3 September The eight from the Annexe are sent to Auschwitz concentration camp in Poland.

1944, October Anne and Margot are taken to Bergen-Belsen camp.

1945, 6 January Edith Frank dies in Auschwitz.

1945, 27 January Otto Frank is freed from Auschwitz by the Soviet Army.

1945, March Anne and Margot die in Bergen-Belsen.

1945, 3 June Otto Frank returns to Amsterdam.

1947 Anne Frank's diary is published.

1960 Anne Frank House is opened as a museum.

1980, 19 August Otto Frank dies aged 91.

Further Information

Books to read

Anne Frank by John Rowley (Heinemann, 1999)

Anne Frank by Rachel Epstein (Franklin Watts, 1997)

Anne Frank, An Unauthorized Biography by Richard Tames (Heinemann, 1998)

Anne Frank Beyond the Diary by Ruud van der Rol and Rian Verhoeven (Viking, 1993) Excellent biography with lots of photos, produced with the Anne Frank House

Anne Frank: Life in Hiding by Johanna Hurwitz (Avon Books, 1999)

Anne Frank, The Last Days of Freedom by Roy Apps (Macdonald Young Books, 1998)

Anne Frank's Tales from the Secret Annexe (Penguin, 1986) The stories that Anne wrote in hiding

Websites

Anne Frank Internet Guide at http://come.to/annefrank has details of many websites about Anne Frank

Anne Frank House at http://www.annefrank.nl

Anne Frank Online at http://www.annefrank.com

Main sources

Anne Frank Beyond the Diary by Ruud van der Rol and Rian Verhoeven (Viking, 1993)

Anne Frank: The Diary of a Young Girl by Anne Frank (Puffin, 1997)

Roses from the Earth: The Biography of Anne Frank by Carol Ann Lee (Viking, 1999)

Anne's quotations in the main text are from *Anne Frank's Diary*.

Index

All numbers in **bold** refer to pictures as well as text.

Anne Frank House 44, **45**
Amsterdam 5, 12, **13,** 21, 40

black market 23
book burning **10**

concentration camps 5, 17, **18,** 33, **40**
    Auschwitz **18, 36,** 38, 40,
    Bergen-Belsen **37, 38, 39, 41**
    Westerbork 33, 34, 35, 36

death camps 25, 35

First World War 7
food **23,** 26, 34, 37, 39
Frank, Anne **4,** 5, **6, 9,** 11, **12, 13, 15, 17,** 19, 21, 22, 24, 25, 26, **28,** 30, **31, 33,** 34, 37, 38, 39, 40, 41, **43**
    bedroom in Annexe **24, 25**
    boyfriends 15, 19, 28, 29
    diary 4, 5, 11, 13, 15, 18, **19,** 21, 22, 25, 26, 28, **30,** 31, **33,** 42, 43
    friends 12, **13,** 17, 19, 24, 28, **29,** 38
Frank, Edith 4, 6, **9,** 12, 37, 38
Frank, Margot 4, **6, 9,** 11, **12,** 13, 19, 22, 24, 37, 38, 40, 41
Frank, Otto 4, **6,** 7, 8, 9, 16, 20, 21, **22,** 24, 32, 40, 41, **42,** 43, 44, 45

Germany 7, 8, 9, 12, 15, 34, 43
    Frankfurt **7, 9,** 10, 11
Gies, Miep 4, 20, **22,** 33, 41

Hitler, Adolf 8, **10**
homosexuals 9, 10

Nazis 5, 8, 9, **10,** 11, **14,** 15, 18
Netherlands, the 11, 12, **13,** 15, 18, 36, 40, 41
newspapers 18, 22

Second World War 15, 40
    Britain 16, 26, 39
    D-Day landing **34**
    Italy 26
    Poland 18, **19,** 35
    USA 16

Secret Annexe 5, 20, **21,** 23, **25,** 30, 40
    bookcase **21**
    toilet **25**
synagogue **8**

religion 7
    Catholics 7
    Jews 4, **5,** 7, 8, 9, 10, 11, 12, **14,** 15, **16,** 17, **18, 19, 27, 32, 35, 36, 37,** 41, 43
    Protestants 7
Romanies 9, 10

Van Pels **20,** 30, 44
    Auguste **20,** 25
    Hermann **20**
    Peter **20,** 25, 28, **29**

Grandma
Forgets

Paul Russell & Nicky Johnston

EK

My grandmother forgets who I am.

Every time we meet, it's like meeting someone new.

'You look lovely today,' says Grandma. 'You remind me of old Sam.'
But we don't know who old Sam is.

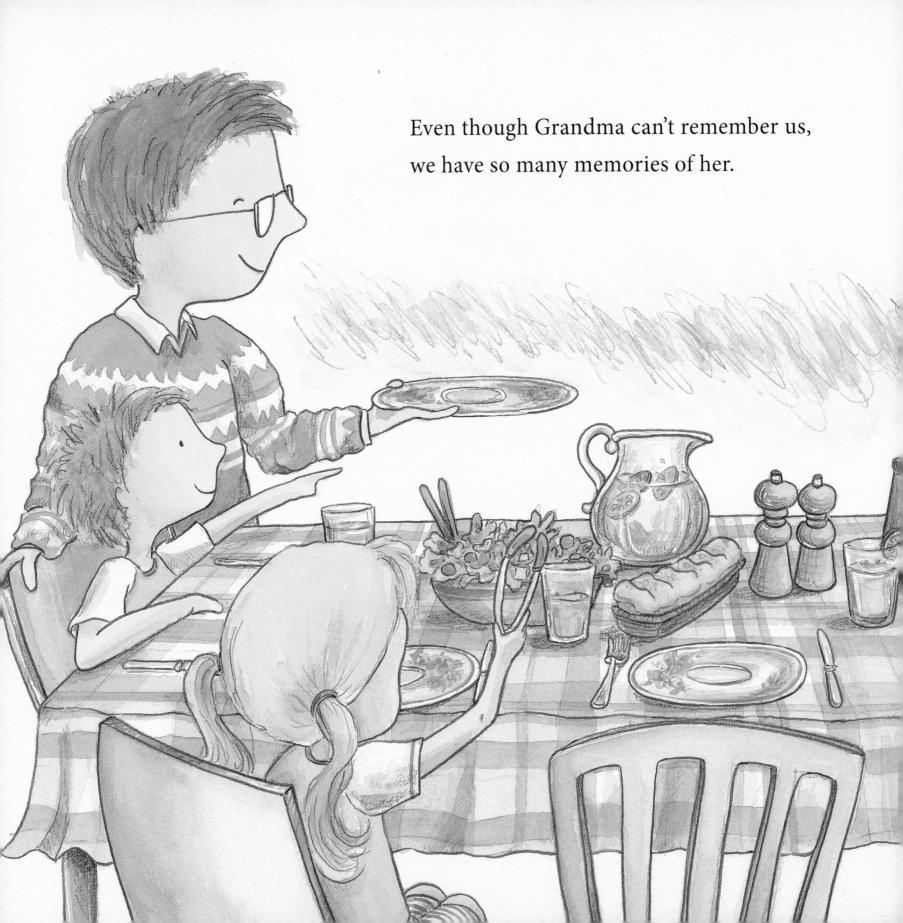

Even though Grandma can't remember us,
we have so many memories of her.

We remember sausages the size of elephant legs, served up for Sunday lunch.

We remember her sky-blue car driving us to the beach.

And piled high with old ladies going to bingo.

We remember a hot-water bottle by our toes in her bed,
thunder crashing outside as she held us tight.

We smell baking apples in the winter
and remember climbing as high as
the sky in Grandma's apple trees.

It doesn't matter if Grandma forgets how to play our games. She still smiles and claps along.

Sometimes she makes up new games.

I like it when she hides Dad's keys.

She jokes she can't remember
where she hid them.

Sometimes Dad is sad because he has to hold onto the memories for both of them now. I help him make new memories that we can share. And remind him of the time he left his jacket on the school bus when he was eight.

Grandma always remembers that too.
Even when she can't remember his name she
still reminds him not to forget his jacket.

Even though Grandma can't remember us,
we have so many memories of her.

Every time I see Grandma I tell her that I love her.
So it doesn't matter if she forgets.

For my nana, Gladys Russell (1918–2007).
— P.R.

For my mum Annie, a grandma who gives
endless love, tradition and fun memories.
— N.J.

First published 2017

EK Books
an imprint of Exisle Publishing Pty Ltd
PO Box 864, Chatswood, NSW 2057, Australia
226 High Street, Dunedin, 9016, New Zealand
www.ekbooks.org

A CiP record for this book is available from the
National Library of Australia.

ISBN 978-1-925335-47-7

Designed by Big Cat Design
Typeset in 18 on 28pt Minion Pro

Printed in China

This book uses paper sourced under ISO 14001
guidelines from well-managed forests and other
controlled sources.

10 9 8 7 6 5 4 3 2